A long time ago, as a little girl, I
all over the world, and often I'
driving everyone crazy fast! Amused by this my
parents thought, why not call me "History" for short?

Since then I've traveled
by land, sea, and air ...

So read this book and
I'll take you somewhere!

Little Miss HISTORY Travels to MOUNT RUSHMORE
© 2013 Barbara Ann Mojica. All Rights Reserved.
SECOND EDITION

Published in The UNITED STATES of AMERICA
eugenus® STUDIOS
P.O. BOX 112
CRARYVILLE, NY 12521
E-Mail: Barbara@LittleMissHistory.com
WebSite: www.LittleMissHISTORY.com

ISBN-13: 978-1492262985
ISBN-10: 1492262986

Little Miss HISTORY™

Travels to

MOUNT RUSHMORE

Barbara Ann Mojica

Illustrations by Victor Ramon Mojica

When you travel to Mount Rushmore
you will see the heads of four of our most
famous presidents carved into the granite rocks
of the Black Hills of South Dakota.

They are from left to right:
George Washington, Thomas Jefferson,
Theodore Roosevelt, and Abraham Lincoln.
Today more than 3 million people visit
Mount Rushmore each year.

The face of Jefferson was planned for Washington's right side, but the rock was poor ...

... so they had to
dynamite it and carve
a new face on
Washington's left side.

The carvings are
scaled to men
who would stand
465 feet tall.

Each eye is
11 feet across!

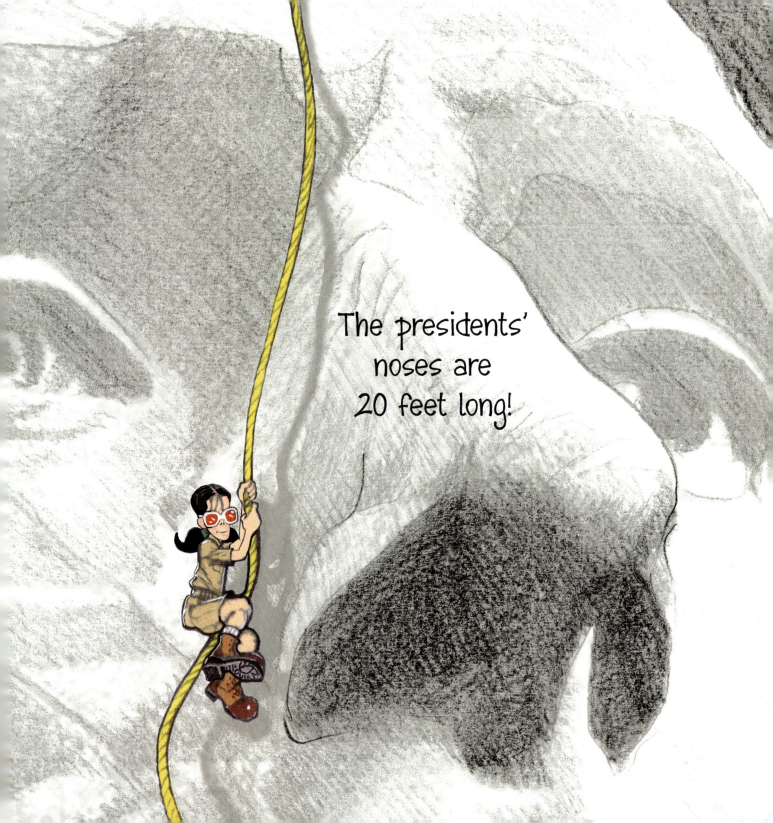

The presidents' noses are 20 feet long!

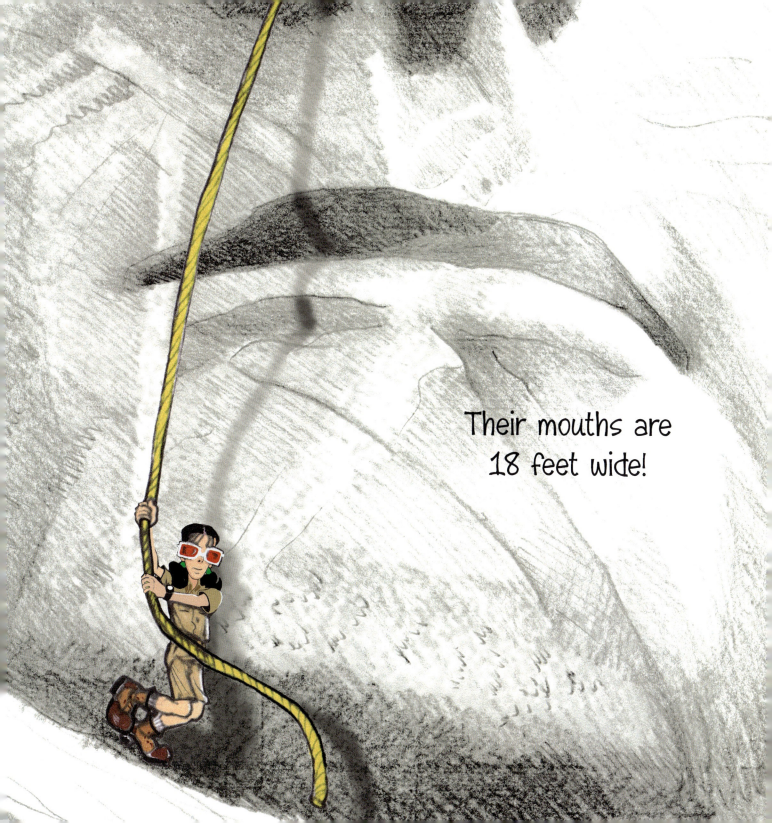

Their mouths are
18 feet wide!

Every worker had to climb 506 steps to reach the top of Mount Rushmore each day.

More than 800 million pounds of stone were taken away. Most of it was removed by dynamiting the rock.

Between 1927 and 1941, Gutzon Borglum and 400 workers carved the 60 foot high faces of each president representing the first 150 years of American history.

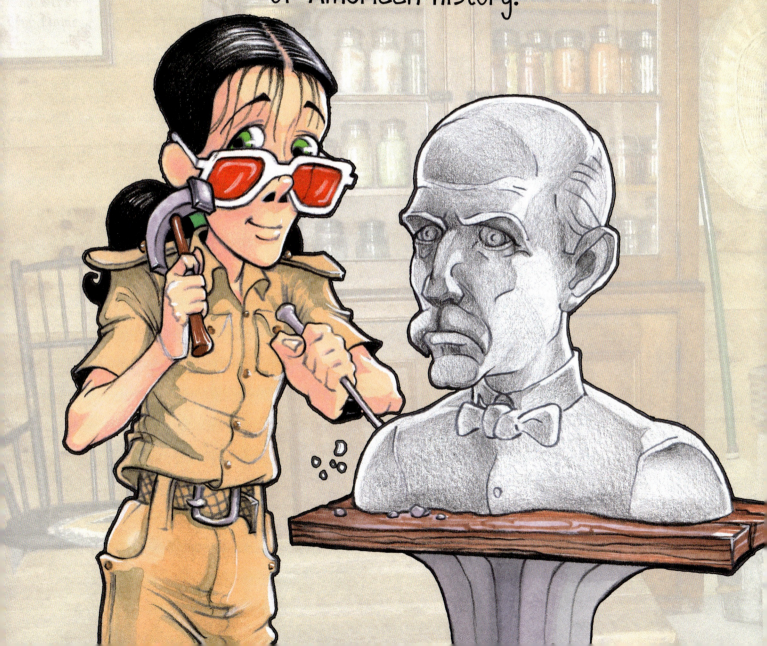

He planned to show them
from head to waist, but he
ran out of money and had to
stop with their heads.

Borglum wanted to preserve the story of our country for future civilizations, but he died before finishing his work.

In 1998, six stone tablets with the words from The Declaration of Independence, the Constitution, and The Bill of Rights, as well as biographies of Borglum and the presidents, were placed inside a teakwood box in the unfinished Hall of Records behind the heads of the presidents.

Many years ago the
mountain was named
Six Grandfathers
by Native Americans
Known as
the Lakota Sioux.

Soldiers of The United States of America took this land after the Great Sioux War of 1876 ...

... even though a treaty had given the Black Hills to the Lakota in 1868.

Now a new memorial is being built nearby to remember this Native American leader ...

... Chief Crazy Horse.
They want to make it larger
than Mount Rushmore!

In May 2012, James Anaya, a Native American activist working with the United Nations, suggested that the United States return the lands around Mt. Rushmore to the Native Americans.

So, What do you think? Who should own the land? Maybe the best idea is to have both monuments honoring Native Americans and the New Americans so we can all visit and remember the history of two great peoples.

Made in the USA
Charleston, SC
30 October 2015